A NOTE TO PARENTS

When your children are ready to "step into reading," giving them the right books—and lots of them—is as crucial as giving them the right food to eat. **Step into Reading Books** present exciting stories or information reinforced with lively, colorful illustrations that make learning to read fun, satisfying, and worthwhile. They are priced so that acquiring an entire library of them is affordable. And they are beginning readers with an important difference—they're written on three levels.

Step 1 Books, with their very large type and extremely simple vocabulary, have been created for the very youngest readers. **Step 2 Books** are both longer and slightly more difficult. **Step 3 Books,** written to mid-second-grade reading levels, are for the child who has acquired even greater reading skills.

Children develop at different ages. **Step into Reading Books,** with their three levels of reading, are designed to help children become good—and interested—readers *faster*. The grade levels assigned to the three steps—preschool through grade 1 for Step 1, grades 1 through 3 for Step 2, and grades 2 and 3 for Step 3—are intended only as guides. Some children move through all three steps very rapidly; others climb the steps over a period of several years. These books will help your child "step into reading" in style!

Step into Reading™

DINOSAUR DAYS

by Joyce Milton
illustrated by Richard Roe

A Step 2 Book

Random House 🏠 New York

For my nieces,
Kirsten and Erica
—J.M.

To my parents
—R.R.

Library of Congress Cataloging in Publication Data:
Milton, Joyce. Dinosaur days. (Step into reading . A Step 2 book) SUMMARY: Brief and simple descriptions of the various kinds of dinosaurs that roamed the earth millions of years ago.   1. Dinosaurs—Juvenile literature.   [1. Dinosaurs]   I. Roe, Richard, ill. II. Title. III. Series: Step into reading book. Step 2 book.   QE862.D5M55   1985   567.9 1   84-17861 ISBN: 0-394-87023-9 (pbk.); 0-394-97023-3 (lib. bdg.)

Manufactured in the United States of America   10 11 12 12 13

STEP INTO READING is a trademark of Random House, Inc.

There are no dinosaurs today.

Not even one.

But sometimes

people find dinosaur bones.

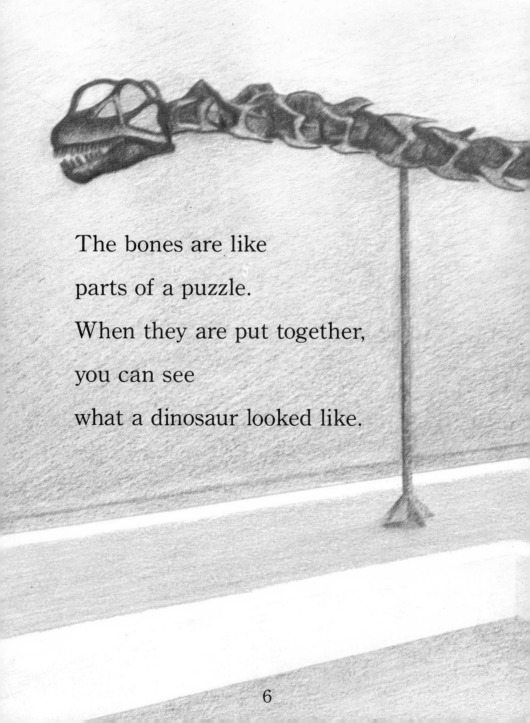

The bones are like

parts of a puzzle.

When they are put together,

you can see

what a dinosaur looked like.

The word <u>dinosaur</u> looks hard.

But it is really easy to say.

Say: DIE-nuh-sor.

<u>Dinosaur</u> means "terrible lizard."

Millions of years ago

the world belonged

to the dinosaurs.

In the days of the dinosaurs

there were no people.

No dogs or cats.

No horses or cows.

What animals were there?

Turtles.

Crocodiles.

Fish.

Dragonflies.

The world was very warm
and very wet.

One of the very first dinosaurs
to live on earth
was named Saltopus.
SAWL-tuh-puss

Saltopus lived near a river.

The river was full
of giant crocodiles.

When these giants got hungry,
they came after Saltopus.
SNAP! went the giants' jaws.
SNAP! SNAP!
Then Saltopus stood up
on its strong back legs
and ran away as fast as it could.

Saltopus was fast.

It could run and leap.

That is how it got its name.

Saltopus means "leaping foot."

Saltopus was a small dinosaur.

About the size of a chicken.

Dinosaurs came in many sizes.

Some were small like Saltopus.

Some were big.

And some

were very, very big.

One of the biggest
was Brontosaurus.
BRON-tuh-SOR-us

This dinosaur was
as tall as a house,
longer than two buses,
and as heavy
as five elephants!

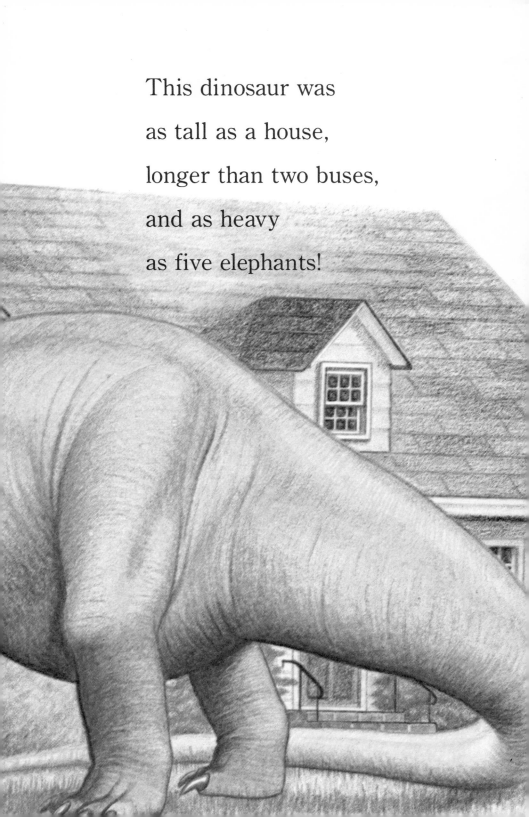

The name <u>Brontosaurus</u>
means "thunder lizard."
When Brontosaurus went walking,
its great big feet
made a noise like thunder.
Brontosaurus ate plants.
Lots of them!

Other dinosaurs
hunted for meat to eat.
One meat eater
was named Allosaurus.
AL-uh-SOR-us

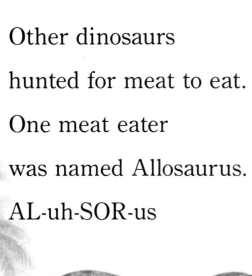

When a hunter dinosaur
came around,
what did Brontosaurus do?
One thing it could do was hide.
Where? Under water!

This dinosaur was fat and slow.

It could not run and hide.

But it did not need to!

Its back was covered
with thick plates.
Its tail was covered
with sharp spikes.
Its name was Stegosaurus.
STEG-uh-SOR-us
That means "covered lizard."
It was one
of the early dinosaurs.

Not all kinds of dinosaurs
lived at the same time.
Early kinds
like Brontosaurus
died out.
And new kinds
took their place.

Some of the newer dinosaurs

looked a little like ducks.

They are called

duck-billed dinosaurs.

This duck-billed dinosaur
is called Anatosaurus.
an-AT-uh-SOR-us
That means "duck lizard."

Anatosaurus had lots of teeth.
Two thousand of them!
It used its teeth
to mash up plants.

What dinosaur

had the biggest teeth of all?

Tyrannosaurus Rex.

tie-RAN-uh-SOR-us REKS

Its teeth were as long as pencils
and very, very sharp.
The word <u>rex</u> means "king."
This dinosaur was the king
of the hunters.
What did it hunt?
Other dinosaurs!

Some dinosaurs

had ways to keep safe

from Tyrannosaurus Rex.

This dinosaur

had hard plates on its back.

The plates were like armor.

When danger was near,

it just sat tight.

The name of this dinosaur

is Ankylosaurus.

an-KIE-luh-SOR-us

Ankylosaurus also had

a strong tail.

It could swing its tail

like a club.

This dinosaur
used its sharp horns
for fighting.
When it came running,
everyone got out of the way!

Its name is Triceratops.

try-SER-uh-tops

That means "three horns on the face."

There are many things

we do not know

about the dinosaurs.

We think most of them

were brown or green.

But we don't know for sure.

Maybe some were brightly colored.

We do know

how dinosaurs were born.

They hatched from eggs,

just like baby birds!

Some dinosaur eggs

were big...

bigger even than a football.

But some were only the size

of a potato.

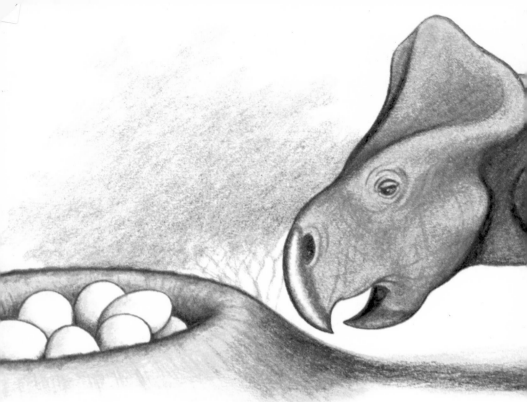

This dinosaur

is named Protoceratops.

PRO-tuh-SER-uh-tops

The mother made her nest in the sand.

She laid many eggs at one time.

Did she sit on the eggs?

Probably not. She was too heavy.

The eggs might break!

When the babies were born,

they were very small.

Much, much smaller

than their parents.

You could hold

a baby Protoceratops

in your two hands.

In the days of the dinosaurs
strange animals
lived in the sea.
They were real-life sea monsters.
Some of these monsters
looked like dinosaurs.

But they were not dinosaurs.

They were called Plesiosaurs.

PLEE-zee-uh-SORS

They had long necks.

They reached into the water

to catch fish.

Other strange animals

flew in the air.

One of these animals

was Pteranodon.

ter-AN-uh-don

Its body was no bigger

than a turkey's.

But its wings were as wide

as the wings of a small plane.

Pteranodon flew far out to sea.

It rested on the tops of waves.

When it took off,

it soared on the wind

like a glider.

The days of the dinosaurs

lasted a very long time.

Millions and millions of years.

Then a time came

when there were no dinosaurs.

What killed them all?

Maybe the world got too hot.

Maybe the dinosaurs could not find

the right food to eat.

Maybe other animals
ate the dinosaurs' eggs.
Some people even think
the trouble was caused
by a comet
that came too near the earth.

No one knows for sure

what happened.

But in time new animals

took the place

of the dinosaurs.

Dinosaur days
were gone forever.